Peggy Fleming: PORTRAIT OF AN ICE SKATER

Other Avon Camelot Books photographed by
Bruce Curtis

WAYNE GRETZKY: PORTRAIT OF A HOCKEY PLAYER

STEPHANIE YOUNG is a writer for *Glamour* magazine. She is a graduate of Stanford University. Originally from California, she now lives in New York City. This is her first book.

BRUCE CURTIS took up photography right out of high school and has been a professional ever since. He specializes in special-effects photography, and creates posters for his own poster company. Bruce is the author of twenty-five children's books. He is the photographer for WAYNE GRETZKY: PORTRAIT OF A HOCKEY PLAYER also available in an Avon/Camelot edition. Bruce lives in Roslyn Heights, Long Island.

Peggy Fleming: PORTRAIT OF AN ICE SKATER

Stephanie Young
and
Bruce Curtis

AN AVON CAMELOT BOOK

PEGGY FLEMING: Portrait of an Artist is an original publication of Avon Books. This work has never before appeared in book form.

7th grade reading level has been determined by using the Fry Readability Scale.

AVON BOOKS
A division of
The Hearst Corporation
1790 Broadway
New York, New York 10019

First Camelot Printing, February 1984

CAMELOT TRADEMARK REG. U.S. PAT. OFF. AND IN
OTHER COUNTRIES, MARCA REGISTRADA, HECHO EN
U.S.A.

Printed in the U.S.A.

DON   10   9   8   7   6   5   4   3   2   1

ACKNOWLEDGMENTS

Line Drawings by Miye Schakne

The photographer wishes to thank:
Grossinger's Hotel, Grossinger, New York
and
Danielle Babayian and her mother, Mrs. Babayian

The author wishes to thank:
Terry Lynn, skating director of Grossinger's
and
Amy Grossman
for their inspiration, information, and
encouragement.

AUTHOR'S FOREWORD

I have been a fan of Peggy Fleming and her ice skating for as long as I can remember—right about the time that I took my first ice skating lessons. I have followed her career—reading about her in newspapers and magazines, seeing her on television—through the years. No matter where or how often I watch Peggy skate, on televised sports programs or at live ice shows, I always come away with the same feeling of admiration and respect for her beauty, her grace, her skill on the ice.

That's why I wrote this book. I felt that the events of Peggy's life and career could serve as a model, furnishing both information and inspiration, for a beginning ice skater. So, I went to the library and dug into newspaper files, read books and magazines about Peggy and her accomplishments. I pieced together major events of Peggy's career (which is still going strong!) and then I added basic ice skating instructions and information. Happy skating!

—Stephanie Young

TABLE OF CONTENTS

Peggy Fleming:
PORTRAIT OF AN ICE SKATER

PART I

SKATING BASICS

CHAPTER 1

Introduction: Ice Skating—Where Dreams
Can Become Reality

You're alone in the center of the ice, poised, calm and ready. The spotlight casts a pale halo around you. The audience sits in hushed silence, waiting for the music to begin. And as the first strains of the music waft over the glistening surface of the ice, you move gracefully, effortlessly into a series of spectacular jumps, spins, leaps and whirls that leave the audience clapping and shouting for more...

Then, the telephone rings, or your mother calls you to set the table, bursting into your star-skater daydream. But it *was* a wonderful daydream while it lasted...

1. Peggy Fleming—Beauty And Strength On Ice

Do you ever wish that you could really skate? Do you try to imagine what it would be like to jump and spin like a pro? To move over the ice with the skill and grace of a champion like Peggy Fleming? You can, if you want. You can make your own dreams come true—but it takes work.

Once, Peggy Gale Fleming was a nine-year-old girl with dreams which she took very seriously. She spent hours on the ice, but she loved skating so much it didn't seem like hard work. And all the time she spent practicing made her ice skating better and better. The same thing could happen to you.

Every single ice skater learns to skate in the same way, first learning the basic techniques of skating, then practicing basic steps, positions, jumps and spins until she can do them well. After that, she must add and develop her own personal style. A skater then combines the basic moves in her own, original way, combined with the music she selects, to express her personality. It isn't the hardest moves that count, but the perfect execution of the simplest moves put together artistically. That's part of the reason why Peggy Fleming was such a winner, because she was such an individual. The way she skated combined exact technique, athletic strength and grace. Peggy won the Gold Medal for figure skating at the 1968 Winter Olympics in Grenoble, France—her ice skating dream—but just like you, she had to start at the beginning.

Your first time on the ice will probably be a lot like Peggy's. You'll look at all the other skaters and wonder if you'll ever be able to do the things they can. You can! Just stick with it.

This book is your guide to ice skating—what the moves are called, what they look like, how they are done. The book starts with very basic moves—maybe you already know them—and progresses to harder, more advanced ones.

This is a book to pull out when you need both ice skating information and encouragement. Plus the story of Peggy Fleming's career will give you a pat on the back and show you what you can do with your dreams. This is a book to study before the 1984 Winter Olympics in Sarajevo, Yugoslavia, February 7–19, or anytime figure skating competition is on TV, so that you can better understand what is happening on the ice. This a book to read and re-read if you're an ice skater. So what are you waiting for? Strap on your skates (in your mind) and glide through these pages!

CHAPTER 2

Equipment: The Right Stuff

Skating equipment—skates and clothes—are important, but they aren't what make a skater great. When Peggy Fleming was working her way up the skating ranks, she didn't own the most expensive skates, wear fancy costumes from special shops or have her hair done at a beauty shop. Peggy's mom made all her costumes and Peggy did her hair all by herself. Once, when Peggy worried about these details, her coach gave her a memorable pep talk. She told Peggy not to be concerned. "Peggy," she said, "You already have the best equipment that money can buy—yourself and your two legs!" Peggy had talent and that talent didn't need dressing up.

What that means is that you shouldn't feel envious of another person's fancy skates. Concentrate on you. If you're not sure about skating, don't get skates you might never wear again. Instead, rent them at your local rink. You can rent them for as little as $2 a session. A session at a rink can last anywhere from $1\frac{3}{4}$ to 3 hours. That's a lot of skating time for very little money! Or, buy a pair of secondhand skates.

On the other hand, if you've decided that skating *is* for you, buy skates—and get the best you can afford. New skates cost anywhere from $35 to $100 and up. What you need to be concerned about most is buying skates that fit correctly. In general, your size in skates runs about a half size smaller than your size in regular street shoes, so don't be surprised if the salesperson tries to fit you with a pair of skates that sound too small. You should always try on skates wearing tights or *thin* socks. Do not wear heavy socks or sweat socks. With thin socks or tights and the proper skate, you will get the correct fit and your feet will stay warm.

Other pieces of skating equipment include:

- **Skate guards**. These are covers for your skate blades. They are made of wood, plastic or rubber and they protect the blades from becoming dull or nicked when not in use. You should put on skate guards whenever you leave the ice. Remember to wipe the blades dry before you put on your skate guards.

- **Blade covers.** These are another kind of blade protector, made from wool or heavy cloth. You'll need blade covers because it's not a good idea to store skates with skate guards on. Skate guards trap moisture and can rust the steel blades of your skates. Remember to remove skate guards from your skates at the end of the day and put on blade covers. When you put away skate guards, place them upside down to drain them of excess moisture.

- **Clothing.** What you wear on the ice is pretty much up to you—just make sure you're warm and can move around comfortably. Look in your closet—you may already have the makings of a skating outfit! You'll need a pair of warm pants with bending room in them, a warm sweater that's not too bulky, a cotton turtleneck, a hat and some mittens or gloves. If you're skating outside, you might want to wear a down vest for extra warmth. Once you are skating, don't be surprised if you feel the need to peel off layers—

you can work up a sweat out there on the ice!

The definite clothing don'ts: parkas, because they're bulky and don't allow you freedom of movement; long scarves, because they can get caught on railings or can trip you; and layers of thick socks, because too many layers can loosen a boot's support.

Once you've discovered that you enjoy skating, you may want to get special skating clothes, such as a short skating skirt or one-piece dress. These clothes give you even more freedom of movement. To warm your legs, pull on a pair of tights and some leg warmers.

CHAPTER 3

On The Ice For The First Time

The first thing to do before you go out onto the ice is to make sure your boots are laced properly and securely. Here's what a correctly laced boot should look like (photo 2).

The laces should be the tightest around the ankle. On most boots, this is where the lacing eyelets (or holes) stop and the lacing hooks start. Snugness at the ankle gives you the support you need for balancing on the blades of your skates and moving on the ice. The laces shouldn't be too tight at the toes. You should be able to move your toes around in the boot—up, down, and sideways. The laces shouldn't be too snug at the very top of the boot. You should be able to slip a finger inside the boot. A little space at the top of the boot will allow you to bend on the ice while your ankle is still supported. The laces themselves

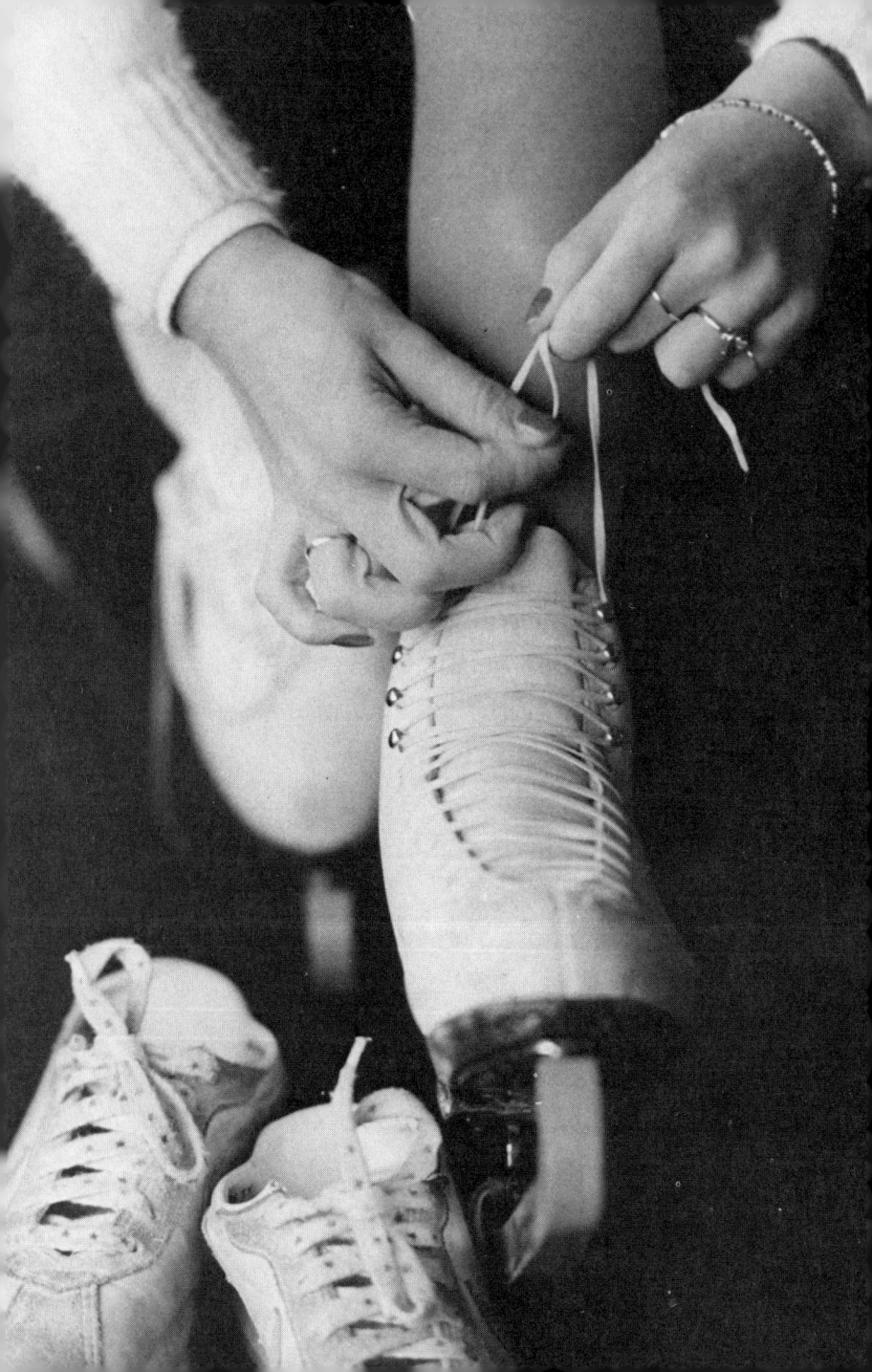

should not be so loose that you can wiggle a finger underneath them, so be careful. A boot will feel like it doesn't fit unless it is laced properly. Another tip: Make sure that any extra lacing is tucked into the tops of your boots, so it does not hang out and trip you. Peggy always laced her left skate first for good luck.

Now that you have your skates on, you may want to hurry up and start skating. But there is something else to do before you can begin: stretching and warming up your muscles. After your first few times on the ice, you'll find out why skating is a sport, just like gymnastics or football. It takes strength to skate, even though it looks easy. Peggy once told a reporter, "That's the whole idea—to make it look easy. Yet I have to move like a track star out there on the ice. All runners have to do is run around a track. Skaters have to work much harder—and do it all in time to music, too!" If you're naturally active and energetic, skating may be just the sport for you. In fact, that's how Peggy started skating. She had so much energy, her mother and father thought an active sport would be a good outlet for her enthusiasm. Before she started skating, Peggy was taking violin lessons. Peggy decided to pursue skating lessons instead because skating suited her active personality.

Pre-Skating Warm-Ups

Before you start to skate try these limbering-up exercises to warm up your muscles. First, stand near the outside of the barrier—the low wall that surrounds the ice rink. You should keep your skate guards on for blade protection as you do this exercise.

With your feet slightly apart, bounce up and down, bending your knees. Swing both arms in front and then behind you at the same time. Your skates don't move, your body does. Pretend that you are about to hop over something. Repeat this movement about five times.

Another stretcher: Face the barrier, holding onto it with both hands. Now, rise up on the toes of your skate guards and then squat down very low. Rise back up onto your toes. Feel the stretch along your legs? You're doing it right!

A more advanced warm-up is pictured in this photograph (photo 3). While on the ice, the

3. A Pre-Skating Warm-Up For Advanced Skaters

skater lifts one leg onto the barrier. She bends over, trying to touch her nose to her knee, keeping her leg straight. Then, she will switch legs and bend again. This kind of stretching should not be tried until you feel more at home and more balanced on the ice.

You'll find that the activities and sports you do off the ice will help your skating. Any sport that requires a bit of strength, some stamina and a solid dose of coordination will benefit your on-ice moves. Peggy loved tennis, golf and water-skiing. In addition, while she attended Colorado College, Peggy took a modern dance class three times a week for stretching exercise and to improve her gracefulness on the ice. You may find that ballet classes or gymnastics do the same for you. Many skaters use these activities to keep them in shape for the ice.

Now that your muscles are all warmed up, you're ready to skate! Take off your skate guards and put them somewhere safe and out of the way, such as under a bench or chair. Now, it's time for the ice.

On the Ice!

If this is your first time or your 50th time on the ice, you should know the basics that follow. Begin by getting a feel for the ice. If you're not used to it, ice can feel very slippery. But this feeling will soon wear off. Hold onto the barrier with one hand and hold the other arm out to your side for balance. Slide your feet—just a little—back and forth on the ice. Then, carefully lift one foot, then the other, off the ice. You don't need to lift your feet very high, just a bit, so you're standing on one foot. Practice this foot-lifting without holding onto the barrier. Keep both arms out to your side —sort of like bird's wings—for balance. Now, try to stand still on the ice, with both feet right under your body. Watch out for other skaters if the ice is crowded. Your best bet may be to pick a solitary corner in which to practice.

Why do these postures? One of the first lessons of skating is to get a sense of balance. Once you do, you'll learn to keep your balance in many positions—even as you're moving, jumping and spinning across the ice.

Good balance makes possible the effortless glides, sharp stops, perfect spins, graceful circles and other special skating moves. *Balance is the key to confidence on the ice.* It comes a little at a time. Each time you're on the ice, your balance will improve.

Your first steps on the ice may be more like walking than skating. That's all right for now. You'll soon learn how to move correctly. Are you ready? Here goes! Bend both knees just a bit, but keep your back straight and your head up. In skating, you'll never stand on the ice with straight legs. If you do, your weight will be unbalanced, too far back on your skates.

Where should your weight be on the skates for the best balance? When you're standing still, your weight should be centered over the middle of your skate blades—right where the arch of your foot is. When you skate forward, your weight should shift just a bit to the back of the arch of your foot. And when you skate backward, your weight should come forward to the front of the foot arch.

In order to move on the ice, you have to learn to shift your weight from skate to skate. Here's a good way to ease into weight shifting. Start with both feet on the ice, spread comfortably apart. (Think of how you normally stand—that's the position you're after on the ice.) Now, raise one foot slightly, keeping your weight balanced on the foot that's still on the ice. Put your raised foot back down on the ice and move your weight forward to that foot. Then you can move your other foot forward. Continue this stepping movement. You may find yourself sliding just a bit. That's all right. Just try to keep your balance. A good way to keep steady is to use your arms. Hold your arms out to either side, with palms facing down toward the ice. Stay close to the barrier so you can grab it for support if you need it. And make sure you're not in the way of other skaters.

Another first move to strengthen steadiness: As you stand on the ice, do a deep knee bend. You'll get the feel of moving up and down while still balancing on your skates. Try a knee bend while you hold onto the barrier with one hand. Then try it without the barrier.

4. Falling—It Happens To Everyone!

Falling

Do you feel better about being on the ice?
Good. There's just one more thing you have to
learn—how to fall. Well, no one really has to learn
how to fall. It happens naturally! And it happens
unexpectedly, as you can see from the photos
(photo 4). Falling is a part of skating. Even great
skaters have fallen. Peggy Fleming has fallen, too.
Once, she fell in the middle of the National Figure
Skating Championships in Vienna, Austria,

March 1966. But she still won the gold medal. What made Peggy come out a winner? She knew how to get up gracefully and quickly and continue skating as if nothing had happened. It didn't bother her and it shouldn't bother you.

When you feel yourself falling, try to sit down on the ice. Bend your knees, let yourself go and try to land on the side of your thighs or fanny. Don't try to stop yourself from falling with your arms or legs; you may hurt yourself. Once you fall, if you're not hurt, get up quickly. You don't want to get in the way of the other skaters. To get up, first roll over onto all fours—your hands and knees. Bring one foot forward so that it is even with the other bent knee. Be sure to put the blade flat on the ice. Stretch your arms to either side of you. Now, you look like you're squatting on the ice. Bring the other foot forward and place the blade flat on the ice. Stretch your arms out in front of you. Rise slowly to a standing position. It's a good idea to practice getting up from the ice in this way so that you know what to do when you fall accidentally. Practice by choosing a spot that's away from any other skaters. Carefully sit down on the ice. Remember, no matter if you fall forward or backward, you always get up the same way: Roll over, put one skate blade on the ice at a time, stretch your arms out and rise slowly to a standing position.

Think of your first few times on the ice as "getting your skating legs," as Peggy called them. She got her skating legs in 1957, when she was nine years old and began her skating lessons at an indoor rink in Cleveland, Ohio. She started with a once-a-week lesson—every Thursday after school. But she practiced what she learned in those weekly lessons every single day.

To make steady progress, you should skate at least two to three times a week for 45 minutes to an hour at a time. You may make progress skating only once a week, but it will be slow going. Most of your time will be spent re-learning your sense of balance and getting it back to where it was the week before. That can be frustrating. Practice your basic moves for balance and soon you'll feel as at home on the ice as you do on dry land! Should you take lessons? Sure— lessons will correct any difficulties you may be experiencing, keep you to a schedule that will mean steady progress and reinforce what you'll be reading about in this book.

CHAPTER 4

Learning To Move Forward

If you've been practicing, you probably feel as if you've mastered stepping and walking on the ice. If you're anything like Peggy, you're itching to get on with it and improve your skating. And it may seem like you have a long way to go, if you watch other skaters skate. Peggy used to watch better skaters on the ice. What she noticed, and what you've probably noticed, too, is that skating consists of continuous movement, each move flowing into the next. Sometimes, it's hard to distinguish where one move stops and another begins!

Sculling

An easy way to begin learning the smooth motions of ice skating is to master the technique of Forward Sculling. Sculling is a method of pro-

5. *A Skater In Motion*

gressing across the ice by moving both feet in and out. When you scull, you're pushing the toes of your skates out and then pulling them back together again. The marks that your blades leave on the ice look like half circles; something like this:

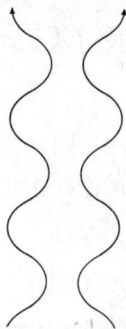

Both your skates should be about eight inches apart when you start the sculling motion. Your arms stay in the same position throughout this movement—out to either side, straight but not stiff. Your hands can be held at any height that's comfortable to you—anywhere from nearly level with your shoulders to down around waist level. Your weight will be on both skates. That way, you won't get out of control or turn sharply to one side. To start, point both toes out, bend your knees and push your skates outward. Let the skates slide out until they are about a shoulder's width apart. Then, slowly turn in your toes and bring both feet back together again. Repeat this push-pull of the skates and you'll skate forward smoothly and continuously. Practice sculling down the length of the rink and back, so you get the hang of it. This is what skating is all about— controlling your skates so you can move across the ice.

Learning to Glide

Now comes the time to learn how to ride your skates, or glide over the ice. Gather up some speed by sculling, then place both skates right under your body (to balance you) and glide. The whole point here is to hold your position, maintain your balance and let the skates take you for a ride. Moving or gliding over the ice is another key part of skating. Keep your arms out to the side of your body for balance. Watch the way you hold your arms. Try, as Peggy did, to look graceful as you glide over the ice.

After you feel comfortable gliding on both feet, try it on one foot. As you glide forward on two skates, lift one skate a few inches off the ice. Lift the skate straight up off the ice. You're now gliding on one foot. Again, your arms are out to your sides, balancing your glide. Practice gliding on both right and left legs by lifting the left or right skate off the ice. Figure skating is full of moves for both right and left skates.

Skating Terms

Skaters use specific terms to describe the difference between the right and left sides of the body. "Skating" refers to the side of the body that's on the ice; "free" refers to the side of the body that's off the ice. Study this photo (photo 5): This skater is skating on her left foot; her right foot is off the ice. Therefore, all the body parts of the pictured skater's left side—foot, leg, knee, hip, shoulder, arm—have the word "skating" in front of them. Her left leg is her skating leg, her left arm is her skating arm, and so on. The right side of her body—foot, leg, knee, hip, shoulder, arm—all have the word "free" in front of them. So her right leg is her free leg, her right arm her free arm, and so on. But, her left side could become "free" and her right "skating" if she switched leg positions.

Since skating involves moves to both the right and left, using both the right and left legs and arms, these labels make the positions of the body clearer. The position of an arm or leg, whether it's a skating arm or leg, or a free arm or leg, makes a big difference in how well you perform skating moves.

When it comes to one-footed skating moves, you're bound to discover that it's easier for you to skate on one leg, say your right, than with your left. It just feels better, more natural to you. And it's not so odd when you think about it. After all, you show a preference for right-handedness or left-handedness. For now, it's best to stick with your natural preferences, but remember: As you improve, you'll have to demonstrate your abilities with both right and left sides. There's no way to know which side is your stronger side until you get out there and skate, so that's another reason these labels are good to know. This book can't guess for you. So you won't get confused by the directions and instructions in this book, "skating" and "free" will be used as much as possible in place of "right" or "left," so you can adapt the information to your own skating style.

A Simple Skating Figure

Once you've mastered lifting one foot off the ice and gliding, try to do something a little bit artistic. Straighten out and extend the free leg (the leg that's *off* the ice) in back of you as you glide. To do this, you may have to lean your upper body forward a little bit, to balance the weight of the leg extended in back of you. This move is leading up to your first free skating position, or figure! It's called a Forward Spiral. The photographs, (photos 6, 7) show you what it looks like.

Not sure about this move? Practice at the barrier first. Stand facing the barrier, holding onto it with both hands. Your arms should be stretched out straight in front of you. Balance on one leg (whichever feels strongest) and extend the other leg behind you, into the spiral position. A tip: Push the heel of your skating foot (the one that's on the ice, balancing you) into the ice for better balance. Let go of the barrier and see if you can hold the spiral position. It takes strength to ice skate! Now, you may be more sure of yourself and can try a forward spiral without holding onto the barrier.

6. *Peggy Starts A Forward Spiral*

7. *Final Position for A Forward Spiral*

When you feel you're prepared, start out with a one-foot glide. Keep your free leg stretched out behind you and try to hold it up high. Point the toe of your free foot out, away from the body and slightly up. Your arms are spread out like the wings of a bird. Arch your back to help you get your leg up even higher. Ideally, the height of your raised leg and shoulders should be even—that's how the pros do it.

Another Forward Movement—Stroking

The next step in your program is to learn skating's most basic move: Stroking. Every skater, from beginner to Olympic champion, learns stroking and uses it through every level of her skating. It's a movement that's used to string one move to another. Stroking is a combination of the skills you learned by sculling and gliding. It is a forward gliding movement in which you change your weight from foot to foot. It's a continuous, smooth movement. The force that moves you forward comes from pushing out with the side of the blade (don't use toe picks, that's cheating.)

Stand with your feet parallel and hip-width apart. Unlike sculling, where you started and moved with your weight on both skates, in stroking your weight passes from foot to foot. Hold your arms out to the side, hands slightly in front of your body. To start, turn one skate so that the toe points out, away from your body. Both boots should now be almost touching at the heels. Keep the blade of your turned-out foot on the ice. Push off against the blade of the turned-out foot (the free foot) and glide forward on your opposite leg, your skating leg. All your weight is on your skating leg. Your free leg should be extended behind you, about three inches off the ice. As you begin to slow down, bring your free leg forward—even with the skating foot—and put it back down on the ice. Now, because you are stroking and shifting your weight from one leg to the other, the leg that was your free leg will become your skating leg and your skating leg will become your free leg. Turn the blade of what was your skating leg out to the side—it is now your free leg. Push off from the turned-out skate and balance all your weight onto the new skating leg.

By repeating this stroking motion, you'll move quickly down the ice. At first, your strokes may be short and choppy, but with practice, you'll learn to make longer, stronger and more rhythmic strokes. For now, concentrate on getting the motion right. It's a good idea to practice stroking for five minutes without stopping. Increase your time to 10 minutes of non-stop stroking. Here's how your blades should mark the ice if you are stroking correctly:

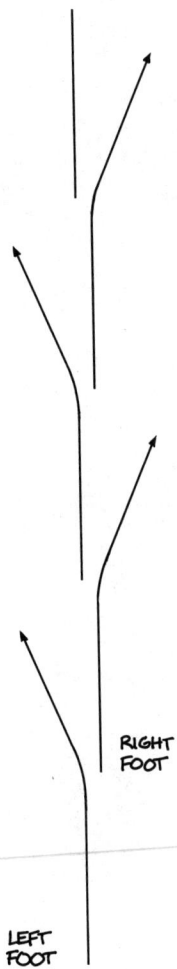

RIGHT
FOOT

LEFT
FOOT

CHAPTER 5

Learning To Stop

Now you know how to move forward in two ways: sculling and stroking. Almost as important as moving forward is stopping. Crashing into the barrier—although a sure-fire method—is the wrong way to stop.

Where are the brakes on skates? The edges of your blades. To stop, you want to scrape the blade lightly over the ice, as if you were trying to shave the surface. Practice "shaving" at the barrier. Facing the barrier and holding on with both hands, bend one skate blade so that your instep scrapes over the surface of the ice. Practice with the other foot, too. Now you have an idea of how to position your skate blades to bring yourself to a stop.

There are several different stops you should know. The easiest way to stop is the Snow Plow Stop. It's just like the stop in snow-skiing. You

8. *A T-Stop*

bend your knees as you slowly push your toes together and your heels apart. Your ankles lean in slightly toward the inside of your skates. Your blades scrape the ice and halt you.

Another stop is known as the T-Stop. It's called this because in the final position, the two skate blades form the letter "T." If you are skating forward on one foot (your skating foot), you bring the instep of your free foot up to the heel of the skating foot as this photo (photo 8) clearly shows. In the photograph, the left foot is the skating foot, the right foot the free foot. As you lower the free foot and blade onto the ice, you slowly shift your weight back onto the free skate, which will bring you to a stop.

There's another graceful movement that is based on the T-stop, called the Lunge. It's a bit more advanced, but it's sure to impress an audience! As you glide forward on your skating foot, in this case the left, (photo 9) place the free foot down on the ice. Now, bend your skating knee deeply and extend the free foot straight out in back of you, dragging it behind you. The drag of the right blade on the ice brings you to a stop

9. *A Lunge Stop*

slowly, but not before you've done a pretty move on the ice. Keep your arms out to your side for balance, keep your head up and smile!

CHAPTER 6

Learning to Skate Backward

Now's the time to put yourself in reverse!

In figure skating, going backward must become as natural to you as skating forward. You'll need to learn to skate backward very early in your training. It may seem strange to be skating without any idea where you're going, and it will take some time to get over this sensation. Skating backward is not as easy as the forward moves you've learned so far. Perhaps you'll want to ask an experienced skater to show you the ropes. Or maybe, you should sign up for a group lesson. If you're going it alone, why not practice at the barrier until you get the hang of it?

Hold onto the barrier with one hand. Step backward, one foot at a time. This will get you used to reverse balance and body position. You might try to push yourself backward along the barrier, to discover how it feels to move backward smoothly. Also, you should practice looking over one shoulder to see where you're going.

When you skate backward, your posture is important. Your head should be up, your shoulders down and relaxed, your back straight, knees slightly bent. Beginners often make two errors that can slow their learning to skate backward: (1) They bend forward from the waist to keep from falling backwards. To counteract this natural tendency, concentrate on proper posture, keeping your back straight. (2) They swing their hips from side to side, thinking it will help propel them backwards. Keep your body in line, and let your legs and skate blades do the work.

Backward Sculling

The first technique to learn to skate backward (without help from the barrier) is by backward sculling. You'll recall that you learned to scull in the forward direction.

To scull backward, stand on the ice with your skates about a hip's width apart. Your arms are in the familiar balancing position, out to your sides. Turn in both toes and turn out both heels. Bend your knees a bit, push back and let your skates separate. As your feet spread apart, you'll move backward. Continue the backward motion by pulling your heels back together and then pushing them out again.

Having a little trouble getting started? At first, you may find that it's easier to scull backward if you're already moving. Try pushing off from the barrier, just to get going. Then begin the backward in-and-out motion of your skates.

There's another way to skate backward, too. This method, a side-to-side push, will prepare you for advanced skating movements.

Stand with your feet comfortably apart (8 to 10 inches), both knees bent, your weight on both skates. Keep your shoulders straight and your arms out to the side but bent at the elbows so that hands are in front of body. Now, turn both heels—at the same time—to the right, by twisting from your waist. Your lower body goes one way, your upper body goes in the other direction—and that's what makes you move. As you twist both heels to the right, your weight will shift to the right foot. You'll feel yourself slide to the right and backward a bit. Twist from the waist again, this time to your left side. Don't stop—keep twisting from side to side (don't swing your hips!) and you'll move backward.

Backward Gliding and Stroking

Another move to practice, once you've learned how to start moving backward from a standing position, is gliding backward. Use either backward sculling or the side-to-side push to build up some speed. Then place both skates underneath your body and ride your skates. Turn your head over one shoulder to see where you're going, and to watch out for other skaters.

Still another backward move to add to your bag of tricks is backward stroking. The term "stroking" should sound familiar. You've already learned how to do forward stroking.

Let's begin with your left foot. Turn out your left heel and push, transferring your weight to the right foot. Lift the left foot (your free foot) off the ice, extending it in front of you. As you glide backward begin to move your left foot alongside your skating foot. When both feet are together, place the blade of the free foot down on the ice. Then push off from your right blade, so that your left foot becomes the skating foot. Repeat this motion again and again. Try to develop a smooth rhythm. Saying these words may help: "Push, together, pause...push, together, pause, etc." "Push" refers to the push-off from one skate or the other. "Together" refers to bringing the feet together, your skating foot on the ice, your free foot just above the ice. When you say the word "pause" your feet should be together, both blades on the ice.

Stopping Backward

You can stop as you're moving backward just as easily as you stop moving forward. The easiest way to stop is by using your toe picks, by learning the One-Foot Scratch. As you move backward on both feet, slide one skate out behind you. You may want to move both arms in front of your chest to counter-balance the weight of your leg behind you. Raise the heel of the skate just enough so that the toe pick scrapes the ice. When the toe pick grabs the ice, you will come to a stop. Just because a one-foot scratch may be one of the first backward stops you learn, it doesn't mean that great skaters don't use it, too. Here (photo 10), Peggy demonstrates the simple, elegant beauty of a one-foot toe scratch.

You can also do a backward Snow Plow to come to a stop. As you skate backward, turn both heels out and squeeze your knees together. The blades will scrape the ice and bring you to a stop. Keep arms out to your side for balance.

A more advanced backward stop is the Two-Foot Toe Scratch. For this stop, you must lift both heels off the ice at the same time, by leaning forward onto both toe picks. As you might guess, this requires good balance and body control to lean forward just enough without falling.

10. *Peggy Performs A One-Foot Toe Scratch*

CHAPTER 7

Summary: What You've Learned So Far

This summary will show you just how far you've come. Maybe you want to refresh your memory on a certain technique—all you have to remember is to turn to the summary to find out where you read about it.

So far, you've learned about standing, balancing, moving forward and backward and stopping on the ice. These are the basic moves of skating. All the other moves in skating—even the most spectacular spins and jumps—are based on these five movements.

You have also been introduced to the step-by-step progression of skating moves. The form and techniques you learned from a basic move provide a stepping stone for more advanced moves. For instance, you first had to learn to

11. Peggy Takes A Bow

balance on the ice. Then you had to get used to the feeling of moving on the ice by sculling. Sculling was important to prepare you for the two-foot glide. After the two-foot glide, you progressed to a one-foot glide. In general, you'll find that the advancement in skating moves from a two-foot to a one-foot move; from a forward direction to a backward direction.

When Peggy Fleming began ice skating, she started in group lessons and was taught these same basic moves. From there, Peggy learned to improve her form and sharpen her skating skills —in much the same way you are.

In order to become a more advanced skater, you'll need group lessons and, perhaps, even individual lessons. Maybe, like Peggy, you will be singled out from your group by your teacher for your special talent and be encouraged to pursue skating competitively. But even if you aren't interested in competition, the advice would be the same: Be the best you can be, take pride in your own accomplishments on the ice and, above all, have fun skating. Peggy skated only to please herself. So should you. (photo 11)

A Checklist of the Moves and Terms Covered in This Section

Just to jog your memory, here are the topics covered so far:

- Lacing Boots
- Pre-Skating Warm-Ups
- Balance
- Falling
- Sculling (forward)
- Gliding (forward)
- "Skating" vs. "Free"
- Forward Spiral
- Stroking
- Snow Plow Stop
- T-Stop
- Lunge
- Backward Sculling
- Backward Gliding
- Backward Stroking
- One-Foot Scratch Stop
- Two-Foot Scratch Stop

PART II

THE FINE ART OF FIGURE SKATING

CHAPTER 8

Learning To Turn

Up to this point, you've been skating in a straight line. That's fine, except that most ice rinks aren't a straight stretch of ice. Instead, they are rectangular areas of ice, 26 to 30 meters wide and 56 to 60 meters long. That means, sooner or later, you're going to have to turn in order to keep skating continuously! You'll discover that skating is a sport of curves, or edges, as they're called technically.

The Skating Edges

Edges are what make skating movements look so exciting, graceful and free. Not only can your body move forward and backward on the ice, you can also lean it from side to side. Your skate blades are specially built to help you achieve curved movements. Take a look at the bottom of your skate blade. It consists of three parts: an inside edge (along the inside of your blade); an outside edge (along the outside of your blade) and the middle (which is actually a groove between the two edges).

As a beginner, you've been skating flat—on both edges of the blade at once. Now, you're ready to skate on one edge at a time. To do this, you shift your weight from outside to inside or inside to outside. Drop your weight to the inside of your foot to skate on an inside edge; to the outside of your foot to skate on an outside edge. Your ankles should not bend when you shift your weight. If they do bend, your boots do not fit properly. Have your fit checked.

There are eight basic edges in skating. You can skate on either the right foot or left foot, forward or backwards; or on either the inside or the outside edge. Here's a list of the eight possible edges:

- the right forward outside edge, usually shortened to *right forward outside* or RFO,
- the left forward outside edge, or LFO,
- the right forward inside edge, or RFI,

- the left forward inside edge, or LFI,
- the right backward outside edge, or RBO,
- the left backward outside edge, or LBO,
- the right backward inside edge, or RBI,
- the left backward inside edge, or LBI.

For the skating moves that follow here, it's important to remember that no matter what the edge, it's the direction in which you are leaning that makes the difference. If you lean to the left, your skate will travel in a curve to the left. The same holds true for leaning to the right. In fact, you'll find that most of skating involves leaning into the center of the curve you want to make. It is very important to learn to lean your body in a single line. Your whole body—from your ankles to your head—must lean into the center of the curve.

Learning edges will keep you busy. You should practice all eight edges so that you can do them naturally. And you should also learn to hold an edge. Holding an edge means to skate on the same edge for a long distance or for a long time. If you hold an edge long enough, you'll eventually curve into a circle.

Holding an edge to create a curve is the basic movement you'll use in skating the School Figures or Compulsory Figures, which will be described later.

The Hockey Glide

One of the fundamental ways to put your edges to work and maneuver around a curve is with a Hockey Glide. Glide forward on both skates, with one foot directly in front of the other. Let's say you're approaching the end of the rink and you want to make a turn. Take the foot that's closest to the center of the turn you want to make, and move that skate in front of your other skate. Shift your weight to the back skate. For example, if you are turning to the right, your right foot is closest to the center of the turn, so you would position your right skate in front of your left, and shift your weight to the left skate. Your right arm is held raised comfortably in front of you; your left arm is raised and extended in back of you. Your upper body is turned away from the center of the curve while you lean forward into the curve. Practice a hockey glide by going around the rink, clockwise and then counterclockwise—so that you can practice with each foot. Each time you come to a corner, turn with the hockey glide.

Crossovers

The only drawback to using a glide to round a curve is that you lose speed at the end of the glide. So that you don't lose speed, the next kind of turning motion you'll need to master is the Crossover. Skaters use crossovers to maintain or even increase their speed on the ice. You'll need speed to do spins and jumps. In a crossover, you'll be crossing the free foot around the skating foot. If you try to step over your skating foot instead of around it, you'll lose your balance. You can do crossovers in either a forward or backward direction.

Practice getting the feel of a forward crossover while standing at the barrier. Raise your right foot off the ice and bring it around, in a circular motion, in front of the toe of your left skate. Hold onto the barrier with one hand to steady yourself. Shift your weight onto the right foot and then lift

the left skate, toe first, off the ice. Bring the left skate around in the same way you did the right. In this picture (photo 12), Peggy is executing a forward crossover. Her right skate is crossing over in front of her left. As her weight shifts to her right foot, she'll bend her right knee and push with the whole blade of that skate. Then she'll cross over with the left skate, repeating the motion. As you can see, during the crossover, Peggy's body leans very naturally to the inside of the curve she is making. This keeps up her balance, her speed and her control. Her arms, held like wings, help her balance, too. And, the movement looks very graceful, something Peggy always strived for during her skating performances.

You can do Back Crossovers in much the same way as you do front crossovers. The difference, of course, is that you skate backward. Your body is in a slightly different position, too. If you're curving to the right, for example, your right arm will be extended behind you, with your left arm raised in front of you. Your head will be turned to look toward the inside of the curve.

In the beginning, it may help to scull backward to get moving—a little speed helps make back

12. A Forward Crossover

crossovers easier to do. Cross your left leg around the toe of the right foot, placing it on the ice just inside your right foot. Angle your right blade out to push off. As you shift your weight to the left leg, pick up your right foot and place it on the ice. Now it can be crossed over again.

What's important to a good crossover motion —forward or backward—is the even rhythm of your legs. You shouldn't glide for too long on one skate or the other. Move your legs continuously, pumping your way around the curves and down the ice. It's great exercise! Crossovers are a little tougher than glides, so it may take a while to catch on. But keep at it!

There are two more turns you should learn: a Three Turn and a Mohawk Turn. Practicing and mastering these turns will strengthen your edge control and also come in handy for more advanced skating moves, such as jumps.

Three Turn

A Three Turn is a turn made on one foot. It allows you to change your direction of travel (from forward to backward or from backward to forward) and to change edges (from an outside to an inside edge, or the other way around). The turn gets its name from the line traced on the ice. It looks like the number "3"—something like this:

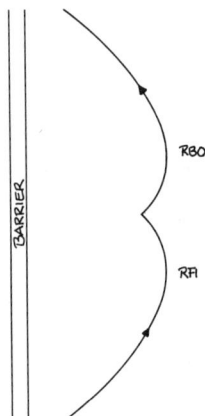

You can practice Three Turns at the barrier. In the beginning, skate in nearly a straight line (instead of the correct curving lines, shown above), just to get used to the feel of changing direction and edge on the same foot. Hold onto the barrier with your left hand. Stand about a skate's length away from the barrier, weight on your right foot, on the outside edge. Extend your free leg (the left leg) out behind you, keeping the toe of the boot about five inches off the ice. Skate forward along the barrier, keeping your left hand in the barrier. Now, bring your right hand to the barrier, turning your upper body to face the barrier. With your skating leg curving to the left on an inside edge, and your upper body twisted to the left toward the barrier, you will find yourself ready to pivot on your skating leg. Let go of the barrier with your left hand, and you will continue on a right backward outside edge. Now, try it on the ice, using just the twisting motion of your body instead of the barrier to make the turn.

Another, more advanced, variation on the three turn is called the Drop or Dropped Three. "Drop" refers to the fact that you change feet and edge after completing a regular three turn. It looks like this:

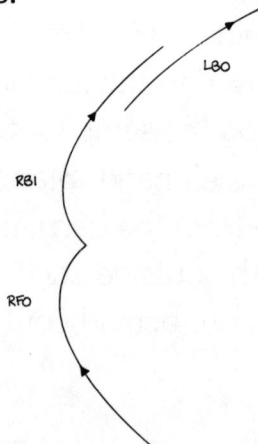

LBO

RBI

RFO

Once you've gotten the mechanics of the three turn down, you can go on to the other turn, the Mohawk Turn.

Mohawk Turn

The Mohawk Turn got its name because it was thought to be similar to a step in the war dance of the Mohawk Indians! The Mohawk is a turn that allows you to change direction, and also to change feet as you make the turn. You do not change edges for a Mohawk turn.

The easiest way to do a Mohawk is from a forward inside edge. Let's say you are skating on a right forward inside edge. As you skate, begin to rotate your upper body to the left (counter-clockwise), as if you were looking into the center of the circle you are making, so that your right arm and shoulder lead the body. Then, turn out your free foot (in this case, your left foot), so that the heel of the boot is positioned next to the instep of your skating (or right) foot. Do not let the skate blade touch the ice. This position should look familiar to you—it's the same position as the T-stop. Once your left foot is in position, transfer your weight from the right to the left foot. You will have changed from a right forward inside edge to a left forward inside edge. After the turn, your right arm remains in the same position, which is now in back of you, since you've changed direction. *Important note:* You should never have both feet on the ice at the same time during this turn. The Mohawk looks like this:

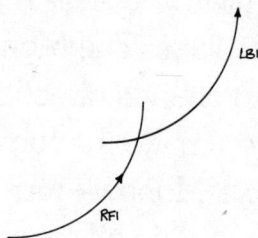

LBI

RFI

Another, more advanced, Mohawk turn is the Drop or Dropped Mohawk. Again, drop refers to a change—in this case, a change of feet as well as a change of edge. This turn starts out as a regular inside mohawk and then is followed by a change of feet and edge to a back outside edge on the right foot. It looks like this:

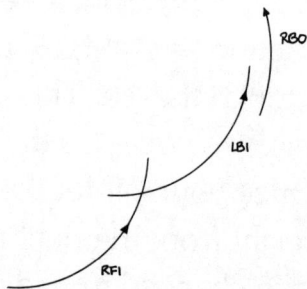

RBO

LBI

RFI

Consecutive Edges

So far, you have learned to hold an edge while you curve around in a hockey glide, You've also learned how to use edges to turn, such as in a three turn and Mohawk. You've also learned to turn while maintaining your speed by executing crossovers. The next step? Turning on one edge, using one foot. For this, you'll need still more control and command of your edges. You'll get that control by practicing and mastering the technique of Consecutive Edges.

In this move, you skate down the ice making half circles, first with your right foot, then your left foot. You skate the half circles using the same edge; a FO (forward outside) edge on the right foot and a FO on the left foot. It looks like this:

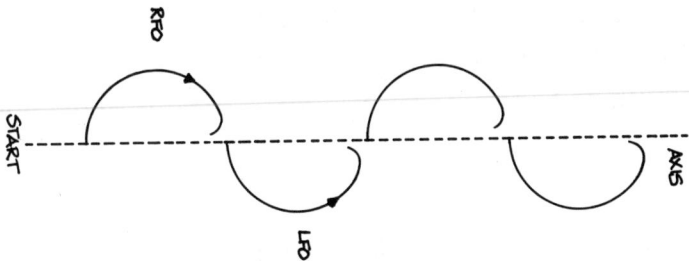

Note that the half circles are centered around a single long line. This is actually an imaginary line called the Long Axis. A good skater can see, in her mind, this long line extending down the ice, and it will help her place her half circles evenly on the ice.

Start your consecutive edges, also called Swing Rolls, in the basic Push-Off Position. In this position, your skate blades form the letter "T." This is the same position as the T-stop. Let's say you want to make your first half circle on an RFO. You start by pointing your right blade forward, in line with the long axis. Your left blade is in back of your right heel—forming the "T." Push off, using the whole of your left blade, onto your right forward outside edge. Your weight shifts to the right (or skating) knee and foot. Your skating (right) arm is held raised in front of your body, pointing to the direction of the curve. Your free leg is extended behind you; your free arm is held raised, trailing behind you. Your head is turned to look into the center of the curve. Keep your chin up, though! About halfway through the curve, bring your free leg forward, parallel with the axis. Your free arm swings forward and your skating arm moves in back of you. Due to the changes in your arm and leg position, your weight will shift slightly to the inside of your skate. This prepares you to complete the curve and return to the axis. When you reach the axis, step off your skating foot and onto your free foot. Make a half circle with the new skating foot, on a forward outside edge.

You can also skate consecutive edges on a forward inside edge. You'll make the same pattern on the ice, but you'll be skating on an inside edge.

You can also do Backward Consecutive Edges, on both the inside and outside edges. The difference between a forward edge series and a backward edge series—besides the direction of travel—is the push off.

To do a push off for a backward edge series, you start with your back to the imaginary long axis. Your skates are parallel to each other, about six inches apart. For a right backward outside edge, for example, raise both arms to shoulder height, then swing both arms to the right. Shift your weight over to the left skate. The power for the push off comes from the inside edge of the left skate blade. Lift the right skate off the ice and place it on the half circle you are going to make. Push off from the left skate—just as you did for sculling—and skate backward consecutive edges.

CHAPTER 9

Learning The School Figures

Once you've learned to skate on all four edges, skate forward and backward, turn and make curves, try to put it all together and skate a circle on the ice.

The skating of circles and other patterns on the ice is the part of figure skating that gives the sport its name. The sharp edges and the curves you create with the skate blade allow you to draw designs on the ice. These designs are known as the School Figures or the Compulsory Figures.

All school figures are based on the shape of the number eight (8). They consist of two or three linked circles. First, you skate a circle on one foot, using a particular edge, traveling in a forward or backward direction, come back to the point you started from, and then skate the same circle again in exactly the same way. Each figure must be skated three times in all. The first circle creates the basic pattern. The next two times around the circle, called tracing, test your ability to accurately repeat the first circle. A technically perfect figure is one in which the three lines are *at most* a quarter of an inch apart! The first time you trace a figure is very important because it sets the pattern for the two tracings that will follow. What do you do when your first tracing is shaped badly? Peggy Fleming answered that question once by advising "If it's just a little out of line, it's better to retrace it. But if the error is drastic, it's better to correct it."

As you have probably guessed, the school figures require good body control, concentration and the ability to stay on a single edge. You've already learned to do these skills, having just practiced edges and consecutive edges.

Peggy worked long and hard on her school figures. When she was competing, in the 1960s, the school figures accounted for 60 percent of her total score in a competition. Freestyle skating (the jumps and spins) counted only 40 percent of the score. School figures were (and still are) always skated first in a competition and if a skater did not score high enough on her school figures, she never got the opportunity to show her freestyle routine to the judges. This never happened to Peggy, because she always scored well in school figures. People have always admired Peggy for her calm determination and quiet concentration. Her coach would tell her that she had a "head for figures!" Today, the scoring in competition is different—skaters perform three school figures that make up 30 percent of their score. Another 20 percent of their score is based on a short program (no more than two minutes long) of seven specified skating moves, such as jumps and spins. Finally, a longer freestyle program (4 minutes for women, 4½ for men) is worth 50 percent of a skater's score.

Even though school figures are a required part of skating, that doesn't mean they are dull or unartistic. School figures allow the skater to show her mastery of slow, precise movements on the ice. Performing the figures requires concentration, strength and patience on the part of the skater. Freestyle skating allows a skater to show her originality, artistry and athletic ability on the ice. Freestyle skating calls for energy, enthusiastic expression and musical timing. Peggy, who excelled in both figure and freestyle skating, liked the difference between the two skills. Each called for a different kind of talent.

You should keep in mind that the school figures are building blocks to more advanced skating moves. Why? How? The figures are curves. And curve skating, curve control and curve accuracy are the skills you must learn in order to master the showy freestyle moves—the jumps, spins and footwork.

Basic Figures

As you'll recall, all school figures are based on a pattern that resembles the number 8, or, as it is called, the figure 8. The Forward Outside Figure Eight is probably the first figure you'll learn. The figure consists of two joined circles. You skate both circles with the same edge of each foot. You start, for example, with a right forward outside edge for the first circle and then switch to a left forward outside edge for the second circle.

How is a figure drawn? How does a skater know how to make the figure? It's up to the skater to sketch the circles herself, using only her imagination and her skates.

One learning aid that is often used as you first attempt to do school figures is an instrument known as a Scribe. It looks like a giant compass, and it is used to draw circles on the ice—much as you use your school compass to draw circles on paper. You use the scribe to draw a circle on the ice. Then, you skate over the circle, following the line that the scribe has made. This gets you used to the mechanics of holding an edge for a complete circle. Eventually, you must learn how to skate a circle without any help from the scribe, for if you skate in a test or other competition, you are not allowed to use the scribe. It's best to learn from the start how to trace, or draw your own figures. For Peggy, the most effective exercise was skating a figure eight in darkness! "That's a real test," recounted Peggy later, "because you can't see if your circle is too long or too wide. You can only imagine it in your inner eye, in your mind."

So, if you can't use a scribe, you must visualize the figure on the ice—see in your mind what pattern you are going to skate. Study the ice and map out exactly where your circles will start and stop and where they will curve. For most of the figures, you will be skating a circle that is three times as wide as you are tall. That may give you some idea of the size of the circle. Another aid comes from the techniques you used practicing consecutive edges. Remember you imagined a long axis? In a school figure, imagine a long axis and then imagine a short axis that divides the long axis in half. Your two circles should meet just where the two lines cross. It should look like this:

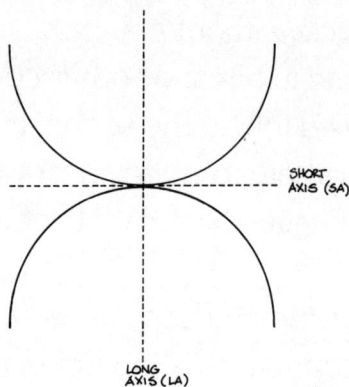

SHORT
AXIS (SA)

LONG
AXIS (LA)

The mapping out of figures on the ice requires a geometric sense of space and distance, and this sense was one of Peggy's great strengths. It developed out of lots of practice and concentration.

When Peggy skated her figures, she thought only of moving her body correctly and placing the figures in a precise pattern on the ice. Nothing else mattered. The only sound she remembers was the crunch of her skate blades as she pushed off to begin a circle.

Here's a rundown of the school figures you'll be learning and hearing other skaters talk about:

Forward Outside Figure Eight (starting to the right)

Stand in the forward push off position (review this position in the consecutive edges section), your skate blades forming a T. The push off is important in figures. It should be a smooth movement, but powerful enough to take you around one whole circle. Bend both knees and push with the entire blade of the left skate. You will skate the first circle on your right outside edge. Your right (or skating) arm is raised and held out in front of your body. Your left (or free) arm and leg are extended gracefully in back of you. Don't try to steer your skate (a mistake beginners often make). Just ride the right outside edge and let the edge follow the curve that it will make naturally. Your job is not to get in the way of this natural curving action! Lean slightly into the circle. About halfway through your first circle, begin to move your free leg to the front of your body. At the same time, without moving shoulders or hips, switch arm positions, so that your free arm moves forward and your skating arm trails back. This keeps up your speed and also prepares you to begin skating the second circle.

Once you've completed the first circle, step onto a left forward edge—without pausing. Your skating arm (now your left arm) is in front of your body. Both the free arm and leg (now your right) trail behind you. At the halfway point of the second circle, move the free arm and leg forward and the skating arm back, so that you'll be ready to skate the figure again. Remember, each figure must be skated three times. Here's what the figure looks like:

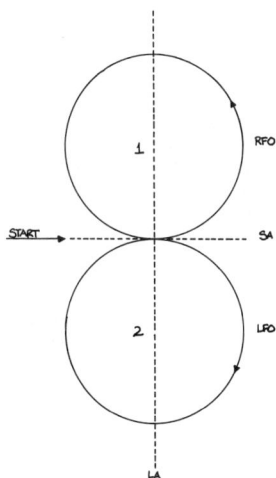

Forward Inside Figure Eight

You use the same starting position for the forward inside figure eight as you did for the forward outside figure eight, except that you'll be skating on the inside edges of each skate. This figure looks just like the forward outside figure eight, but it tests your mastery of the inside edge. The same arm and leg switch positions occur in this figure, too. It can be sketched and summarized as follows:

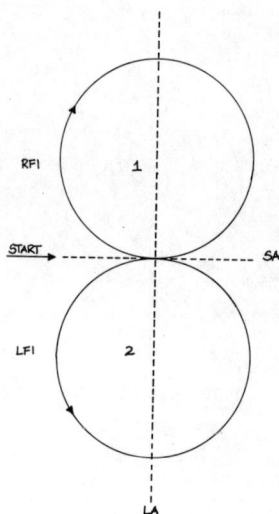

RFI 1

START → SA

LFI 2

LA

Backward Outside and Inside Figure Eights

The figure eight can also be skated backward. The pattern traced on the ice is exactly the same; what differs is the push off. For a backward figure eight, begin with your back to the circle you are about to make. Your feet are parallel to the imaginary short axis. Move the skating foot onto the curve of the circle and push off with your free skate. The free leg is extended in front of your body. Your skating arm is held raised behind you, pointing toward the direction which you are moving. Your free arm is raised over your free leg. Halfway through the first circle, you reverse the positions of the free arm and leg with the skating arm. All the while, you'll be looking where you're going. It is best to look along your skating arm. That way, you won't twist your body out of line. The patterns of the two backward figures look just like their forward counterparts.

Waltz Eight

Building on what you've learned in the basic figure eights, you are now ready to learn a variation. It is known as the Waltz Eight. This figure has two parts: a forward outside edge, and a back inside edge connected by a three turn, which you learned earlier.

When you skate the waltz eight, your starting position, as in other figure eights, is the point where the two circles touch. You should position your Three Turns (one in each circle) about halfway through the circle. The Three Turns in each circle should be on the same line, placed at the same point in each circle. It's best to line them up with the long axis. Here's what it looks like:

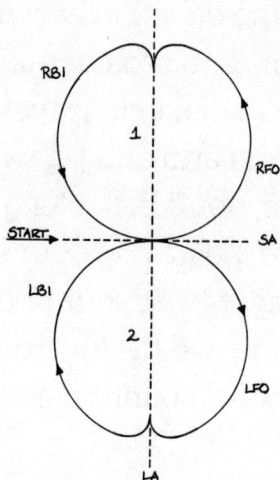

In the waltz eight, you'll change direction for each circle and change feet in each circle. Your free arm and leg switches with your skating arm and will change accordingly.

Another, more advanced version of the waltz eight is called the Double Three. For this figure, you need to position two three turns in each circle. An easy way to space your turns is to think of the circle as the face of a clock. Your starting point is at 6 o'clock. Your first three turn comes at 10 o'clock and your second at 2 o'clock. It looks like this:

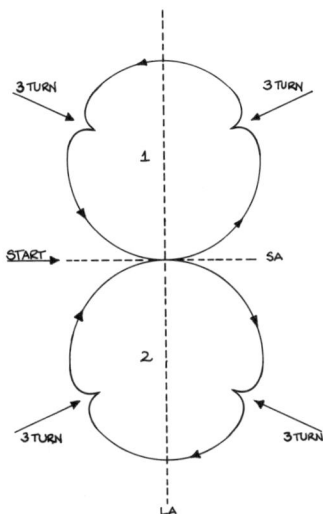

3 TURN   3 TURN

1

START →   SA

2

3 TURN   3 TURN

LA

More Advanced School Figures

The figures that are described below are shown for reference, so you can get a sense of the step-by-step progression of skating. Applying what you've learned from beginning moves to more advanced moves is an important lesson of skating. Be patient, you'll get there.

The Bracket

The Bracket is another figure with a turn in it. The turn itself is just the opposite of a three turn. It looks like an inside-out three on the ice, something like this:

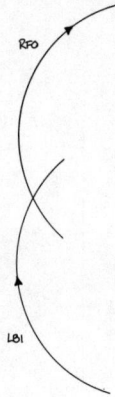

The bracket turn allows you to change from one foot to another, one edge to the opposite edge and one direction to another. The bracket figure looks like this:

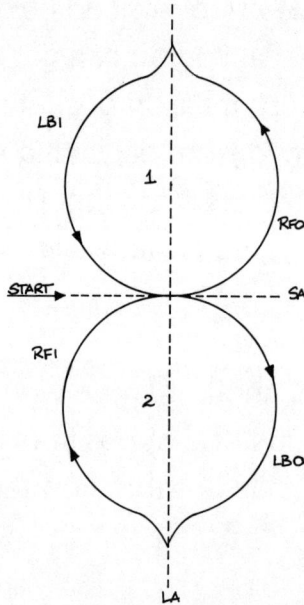

Three-Lobed Figures

Three-lobed figures—a lobe means a circle—consist of three linked circles. They are:

The Serpentine

The Serpentine figure is a combination of the forward outside and the forward inside figure eights. You begin in the same position as the forward outside eight—on an outside edge. For the serpentine figure, you keep your free foot extended in front of you instead of in back. You skate the first half of the first circle on an outside edge. As you cross the long axis, you change edges and skate the second circle on an inside edge.

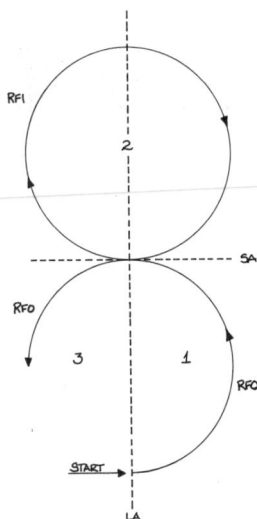

Note the "s"-shaped curves you make going from the first circle to the second circle—that's the serpentine:

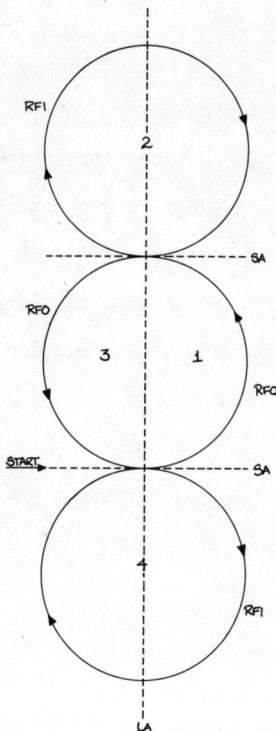

When you've finished skating the second circle on the inside edge and cross the long axis again, switch edges and complete the circle on an outside edge. After crossing the long axis again, you skate the last circle on a right forward inside edge.

The Rocker

In the Rocker figure, you must skate three circles, placing two Three Turns in the two places the circles touch each other, like this:

You can skate an outside or an inside rocker figure.

The Counter

The Counter is another three-lobed figure with two bracket turns placed along the long axis, so it looks like this:

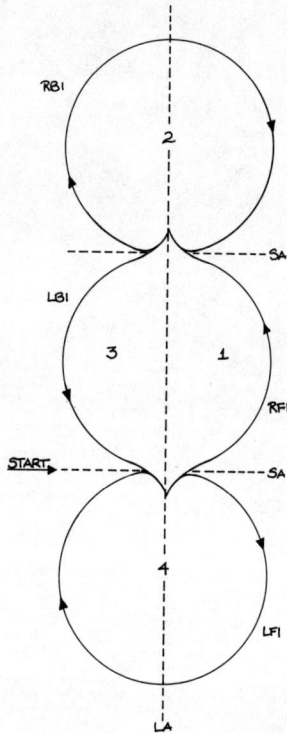

The Loop

The Loop figure most resembles the basic figure eight, but it is much smaller than the other figures you will learn to skate. In the figure, you skate a smaller circle inside. The larger circle should be about three times the length of the skater's foot; the inner loop should be as long as the skater's foot. You can skate both forward and backward loops, the loops on both an inside and an outside edge. It looks like this:

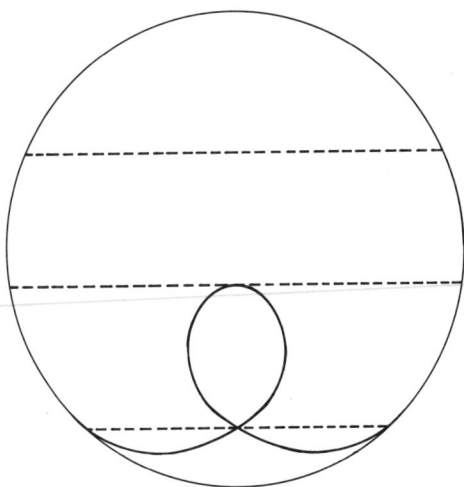

The Paragraph Figures

The Paragraph figures require the skater to skate an entire figure on one foot from just one push off. You can skate a paragraph eight, a paragraph waltz eight, a paragraph loop and a paragraph bracket. In addition, you can skate a paragraph figure on either edge, and in either direction. As you can guess, the possibilities are numerous!

CHAPTER 10

Summary: What You've Learned So Far: Plus, Applying What You Know

From the school figures, you've learned how to control and maintain all eight edges, how to control your speed, how to glide and curve, how to develop steadiness of edges. You've learned how to work your arms and legs to generate speed and motion. You've also gotten a taste of the concentration, discipline and body control that skating requires.

All these skills are important for good form in the school figures. But they are also key to your advancement in skating. These skills are the foundation of freestyle skating—the jumps, turns, spins and fancy steps.

A case in point: In figures, you learned to glide as well as to control the various skate edges.

Now you can apply that knowledge to a freestyle move, known as the Spread Eagle. This move is done with your toes pointing out in opposite directions. Both your skates are on the same edge and you glide over the ice along a curve. It looks a little like a ballet position, except you're in motion. You can do an inside spread eagle (both skates on an inside edge) or an outside spread eagle (both skates on an outside edge).

One way to get into the spread eagle position is to start by gliding forward on one foot, for example on the left forward inside edge. Then, turn your right foot so that the heels of your skates face each other. Shift your body weight onto the right skate, so that your weight is balanced evenly between both skates. Lean into the circle you're making. You're doing an inside spread eagle! In the inside spread eagle, you'll be facing into the center of the circle. In the outside spread eagle, your back will be toward the center of the circle. Be sure to practice the spread eagle on your outside edges, as well.

Another slightly more advanced version of the spread eagle move is the Bauer. It was named after Ina Bauer, the women skater who first per-

13. Peggy Executes The Bauer With A Partner.

formed it. In this position, the toes are turned outward, as in a spread eagle. The difference in the Bauer is that one skate is on an outside edge and the other is on an inside edge. Like the spread eagle move, the Bauer is a movement that can be skated alone, but in this picture, (photo 13) Peggy performs the Bauer with a partner. Notice she is skating on a left outside edge and a right inside edge.

Now that you can see how figures can help with your freestyle moves, let's get started with the second part of figure skating: Freestyle.

A Checklist of the Moves and Terms Covered in This Section:

- Skating Edges
- Hockey Glide
- Forward Crossovers
- Backward Crossovers
- Three Turn
- Mohawk Turn
- Consecutive Edges
- Forward Push-Off Position
- Backward Consecutive Edges
- Backward Push-Off Position
- School Figures
- Forward Outside Figure Eight
- Forward Inside Figure Eight
- Backward Outside and Inside Figure Eights
- Waltz Eight
- Double Three
- Bracket Figures
- Serpentine Figures
- Rocker
- Counter
- Loop
- Paragraph Figures
- Spread Eagle
- Bauer

PART III

FREESTYLE SKATING MOVES

CHAPTER 11

Freestyle Style

Freestyle skating is what many people think makes skating an art as well as a sport. And to some extent, an individual's freestyle skating ability and creativity is what separates good skaters from great skaters. How a skater performs freestyle is a function of that skater's personality, attitude and inspiration. That's what makes a skater like Peggy Fleming stand out. She skates the same jumps, spins, spirals, spread eagles and steps as every other skater, but the way in which her personality, her special style and flair are expressed through her skating makes her a champion. Before Peggy could develop her own freestyle techniques, she had to master the basics of skating.

As you begin to learn the freestyle skating moves, be natural. Let your own personality shine through—it's what makes you unique from all the other skaters. Let your face and body show your feelings. You can study another skater's styles, but think about being yourself on the ice.

As Peggy progressed in her skating, she often asked herself, "What do I want to look like on the ice?" Her answer to that question? She wanted to look pretty and graceful on the ice. She wanted to look like she loved skating. Also, she wanted her audience to enjoy her skating. (photo 14).

The skating style that Peggy developed combined all three of her goals. Her flowing, ballet-like movements made her look very graceful and pretty on the ice. Her hands and arms seemed to express her feelings. Her smile told her audiences how much she loved skating. And because Peggy looked so happy, so natural, so right on the ice, audiences enjoyed her performances.

These are some of the qualities that make Peggy's style different from the style of any other skater. You can see these same qualities in her skating even today. These pictures, from a recent ice show at Radio City Music Hall in New York City (photos 15, 16, 17) show how graceful and

15. *Use Your Arms To Express Yourself*

beautiful Peggy is on the ice. Peggy developed a style that worked for her, and so can you.

Will you ever be able to achieve what a great skater like Peggy has? That's really up to you. Master the beginning steps first, and you're on your way to greatness. If you're just starting out, don't get discouraged that you're still working on so-called beginner's steps. The simple moves that you learn, practice and perfect, will help you learn more complex moves later on. Remember, Peggy started out just like you're doing.

At this point, on the horizon of learning free-style spins and jumps, you may want to take formal instruction from a teacher who gives individual or group lessons. The moves to be discussed in this section are hard to learn all by yourself. A teacher can be a real help—"spotting" or watching you perform these advanced moves. He or she can tell you if your arms, legs and body positions are correct, so that you learn these moves correctly and quickly. In her competitive career, which spanned 11 years (1957-1968) Peggy had nine teachers and coaches and learned from every single one of them. You never stop learning in skating!

One of her most famous coaches was Carlo Fassi, an Italian figure skater who coached her to her Olympic gold medal in the 1966 Olympics in Grenoble, France. In fact, Peggy was the *only* American to win a gold medal at those Winter Olympic Games! Carlo has also coached other skating greats, such as Dorothy Hamill, John Curry and Robin Cousins.

17. Graceful, Flowing Arm Movements

CHAPTER 12

Learning to Spin

A spin is a skating move that twirls your whole body around and around on the same spot. You'll find that when it comes to spinning (and later on, jumping), you will naturally prefer to spin in one direction, just as you naturally prefer to eat and write with one particular hand. In general, a right-handed skater will rotate her spins to the left (or counterclockwise). A left-handed skater will rotate her spins to the right (or clockwise). Go with whichever direction feels the strongest—you'll need all your confidence now. Remember, as you get better, you'll have to demonstrate you can spin in either direction.

A spin consists of three parts: the start or entry, the turning and the finish.

All three parts of a spin are done together in a flowing, continuous manner. There are several

18. Beginning A One-Foot Spin

categories of spins: upright (in which you stand straight on the ice), crouching (in which you crouch on the ice and spin) and horizontal (in which you bend from the waist so that one part of your body is horizontal to the ice). You can do a spin on one or two feet. You can also spin backward.

When you spin, you are turning on a fixed point on the ice—the "center" of the spin—for at least six revolutions. When you're just beginning to spin, two or three revolutions is a very good start. There are two ways to tell if a spin isn't centered; that is, if your skates aren't turning on a single point. First, if you can't increase your speed, and the second, if your skates travel, leaving a mark like a corkscrew on the ice.

Your arms play a key role in a spin by helping you to increase or decrease the speed at which you are turning. When you begin a spin, your arms should be in a basic balancing position—out to either side. To speed up the spin, move your arms in close to your body, by first bringing your arms down to your sides. Then, bring them up to your chest, as if you were trying to hug yourself.

This arm position is the one you will use in most of the spins described here. To finish a spin, your arms are out to either side, in the balancing position, with your free leg extended in back of you.

The Two-Foot Spin

A Two-Foot Spin is performed on both feet. It can be started from a standing position on the ice.

Stand with both feet comfortably apart. If you're spinning to the left, for example, place your left toe pick on the ice. To achieve enough force to get your body turning, you have to wind up. Crouch down slightly, bending both knees, swing both arms to the right, and put your weight on the right skate. Then, quickly swing your arms and twist to the left. Straighten your knees and place your left skate flat on the ice. You will spin in a counterclockwise direction, on the flat of both blades. In your first attempts at spinning, you may only complete one or two revolutions on the ice. Be sure to practice moving your arms smoothly from the balancing postion to the hugging position.

As you're practicing this first spin, you will probably feel dizzy. You will get over this feeling! Never close your eyes during a spin—it will only make you more dizzy. You'll find that the best way to spin is with your eyes open, looking straight ahead. As you come out of a spin, try to focus your eyes on an object straight ahead of you—a post, a door, or someone's face. You'll find you won't get as dizzy if you stare at something that's standing still. With some time and practice, you'll spin better and get less dizzy.

The One-Foot Spin

The natural progression in skating, as you've seen before, is from a two-foot move to a one-foot move. The same progression goes for spins. A One-Foot Spin is trickier—and tougher—than a two-foot spin. Hang in there, you'll get it. Once Peggy learned how to spin, it was her favorite move.

At first, you can get used to the feeling of spinning on one foot simply by picking up one skate—just off the ice—as you are doing a two-foot spin. If you feel yourself wobbling, you can put your foot down on the ice.

Once you've gotten a feel for spinning on one foot, you should learn the proper way to enter a one-foot spin. Entering a spin refers to the steps a skater executes in preparation for the spin. These approach steps—forward crossovers, backward crossovers and other dance steps—help build up a skater's speed and rotation going into the spin.

For a one-foot spin, begin by doing some clockwise backward crossovers to build up some speed. Then, step onto the forward edge of your left skate. Bend your left knee and shift your weight forward onto that leg. As you start to curve around to the left, let your right (or free) leg swing off the ice, in a wide arc.

See how Peggy does this, (photo 18). Swing your free arm around as you spin to the left. Straighten your left (or skating) knee and bring your arms into your chest. You're spinning! As you continue to spin, slowly bring your free leg close to your body, in front of your skating leg. Bend your free leg so that the heel of the free foot is in front of the skating knee. In this position, your legs form the number "4." Your arms should be hugging your body. To increase your spinning speed, straighten and push your free leg down. This takes lots of practice. To exit, or finish the spin, open your arms out to your sides and bring your free foot down on the ice. Shift your weight to your free foot. As you switch feet, you'll stop spinning.

The Sit Spin

The Sit Spin is a spin that's easy to identify. Instead of spinning in the upright position as you did for the one-foot and two-foot spin, in this spin, you crouch down and spin in what looks like a sitting position. You can progress to the sit spin very naturally, after you have learned how to perform both the one-foot and the two-foot spin.

The sit spin was Peggy's favorite spin when she was taking her first skating lessons in Cleveland. She would spin on one foot as fast as she could, and then crouch down and continue to spin in the sitting position. Once in a while, she would lose control (remember, she was still learning) and sit down on the ice. One time, she sat down and slid all the way across the ice—stopping at

19. Step One of A Sit Spin

another skater's feet! It's all a part of learning to skate.

If the sitting position of the sit spin seems awkward to you, you can practice it off the ice before trying it on the ice. Sit in a chair or on a bench. Lean your upper body forward from the waist. Lift one leg so that it is stretched out straight in front of you. Hold onto the knee of the stretched-out leg, lightly with both hands. You are now in the correct sit spin position.

The next stop is to practice the sit-down movement on the ice. The following routine should get you in shape for the sit spin. Skate forward. Stretch one leg out straight in front of you, with the blade about 10 to 12 inches off the ice. Keep your arms out to either side, at shoulder level. Bend your upper body forward and slowly bend the skating leg to sit down, still keeping your other leg out in front of you. Once in the crouching position, squeeze your thighs together for stability. Continue skating forward. Now, try to stand back up. It takes a bit of muscle! If you need a boost to get back into the

upright position, push both hands down against the thigh of your skating leg and stand up.

Once you've practiced these preliminary exercises, you're ready for the real thing. You start a sit spin the same way you begin a one-foot spin. Begin with some backward crossovers stepping onto a forward edge. This time, instead of tucking your free leg in close to your body, keep it extended, a little in front of your body. The free leg is ready to swing into position as you crouch down into the sitting positon. The free leg helps you keep your balance as you crouch (photo 19). The actual crouching, from an upright to a sitting position, is done quickly. As you crouch, keep your arms in the balancing position (photo 20). When you are completely crouched down, move your arms to the front so you can grasp your free leg. Remember, as you bend your upper body forward from the waist, keep your head up. This is what a sit spin looks like, just before the final position is reached (photo 21).

Your goal in the sit spin is to lower yourself so that you are almost sitting on the heel of your skating foot. As you lower yourself, shift your

21. A Sit Spin—Nearly There!

weight forward to help keep your balance. You exit the sit spin by standing up.

The Layback Spin

The Layback Spin has become Peggy's trademark move on the ice. It's an upright spin that is done on the flat of one blade with the upper body bending back. Peggy considered it her special move because she could lean back so far, as you can see (photo 22).

As you swing your free leg around, instead of keeping it in front of your skating leg, let it drop back behind the skating leg. Arch your upper body back gracefully. When you first attempt this spin, you may find it easier to keep your arms stretched up, over your chest for balance, to offset the feeling of leaning back. Once you've become accustomed to the feel of this spin, you can drop your arms down to either side or in back of your body. The arm position is a very expressive part of the layback spin. In these pictures (photo 23), note how Peggy bends her free leg back a bit and stretches her arms back to make a beautiful arch with her body (photo 24).

22. *The Layback Spin—Peggy's Trademark*

23. *Another Layback Spin*

The Camel Spin

You'll probably recognize the look of the Camel Spin because it is similar to the forward spiral position you've already learned. This spin is performed on one foot in the spiral postion. It is a horizontal spin, because the upper body stretches out over the ice. Once again, you enter this spin the same way you did for a one-foot spin. See

24. A Layback Spin—You Can Do It, Too!

how the basic moves let you accomplish the more advanced moves? That's the beauty of skating!

As you enter the spin on a forward outside edge, your free leg is extended in back of your body, your skating knee is bent and your arms are out to either side (photo 25). Now, instead of bringing the free leg in close to the body or in front of the body, it remains extended in back of

you, in the position of the forward spiral. By swinging your arms and straightening your skating leg, you will start spinning. There are many versions of this spin because there are numerous ways to hold the head, arms and body during the spin. In this picture (photo 26) Peggy's body position is "turned out" that is, her upper body is facing away from the center of the spin.

Another variation of the camel spin is the Flying Camel Spin, or the Flying Camel. You enter this spin on a forward edge and exit from it on a backward edge in the camel position. The change from forward to backward edge is done in mid-air! You land on the ice and spin. The "Flying" refers to the edge changeover in the air.

Speaking of flying spins, or spins performed in the air, you can also do a Flying Sit Spin. This spin begins as a one-foot spin. Your free leg kicks out and forward, as you jump into the air. You land on the ice and spin in the crouching position.

There are many spin combinations that put together two or more different spins. Spins can also be combined with jumps and other skating positions. You can rotate from a sit spin to a

25. *Entering A Spin*

standing spin. Or, go from a standing spin to a sit spin. You can switch from a camel spin to a one or two-foot standing spin. These are only some of the possibilities. The only limit to the number of combinations are your command of the movements and your imagination. Go for it!

CHAPTER 13

Learning to Jump

Having learned to spin your body while keeping your balance on the ice, you can now begin to
experiment with jumps. Practically all jumps in
skating require some turning of your body in the
air, so that learning spins is a good way to prepare yourself for learning jumps.

There are two types of jumps: Edge Jumps
and Toe Jumps. In an Edge Jump, the skater
takes off from the edge of the skate blade and
lands on the same edge in which she started. Toe
Jumps are also done from an edge of the skating
blade, but with a little help from the toe pick of
the free foot. As with spins, you may find that
you prefer to jump off from one leg more than
the other. If you feel you can jump higher and
stronger off your right leg, then practice your

27. *A Picture-Perfect Landing From a Jump*

jumps from that leg. It's important that you use the same leg both to jump and spin. Otherwise, you'll have trouble combining jumps and spins. The moves won't flow into each other because you'll have to change legs.

Like a spin, a jump consists of three parts: the start or approach, the in air-motion (usually a turning of the body) and the landing or finish.

All three parts of any jump are performed in a smooth manner so that the move seems continuous. Your arms and free leg help lift you into the air. The position of your body should be upright, with your feet underneath you. Body position is also important for form and appearance. A jump is a special move and should be performed with grace and style.

The Bunny Hop

The first movement you have to get used to in jumping is the feeling of leaving the ice and landing back on it. The Bunny Hop is a good first jump. It is a simple, forward leap from the flat of one blade to the toe pick of the other skate, and then back onto the flat of the first blade. Even in this simple jump, you will learn the special jumping skill of springing up and off the ice.

Let's say you are going to take off from your left foot. Start with your left leg bent. It acts as a spring. You'll jump straight up and off the left leg. Your arms are out to either side and when you make the initial leap off the ice, you'll want to raise them over your head, to help you lift off. In the air, you will kick your right leg forward in preparation for landing on it. You'll land on the toe pick of your right skate. To cushion your landing, bend the right leg as you come down onto the ice. Now, push off from the right toe pick immediately onto the flat of your left blade. Your first jump! Congratulations! Practice jumping from your right foot to your left toe pick and back to your right foot, too, before you move on to other jumps.

It's a good idea to practice your jumping on and off the ice. Off the ice, you can practice jumps on a trampoline, which will also help you get a feeling for height and turning in the air. If you can't use a trampoline, you can always practice jumps on the floor. Better do this on a ground floor—you don't want your parents to think the ceiling is caving in! Clear a space so you don't bump into any furniture. Or, practice your jump techniques on the lawn, where the soft grass will cushion you if you tumble, and mom won't ask if a herd of elephants is in the house!

The Waltz Jump

The bunny hop helped you to practice your takeoff and your landing techniques on the ice. But the bunny hop has no middle—no turn—to it. The Waltz Jump does have a turn—a half turn or revolution, in the air. In this jump, you take off from a forward outside edge, jump up in the air and move your body around a half a turn. What's a half turn? Well, if you're facing a mirror and you turn your back to the mirror, you've rotated your body a half turn. That's what you do in the air in a waltz jump. You land on a backward outside edge of your opposite foot. It looks like this:

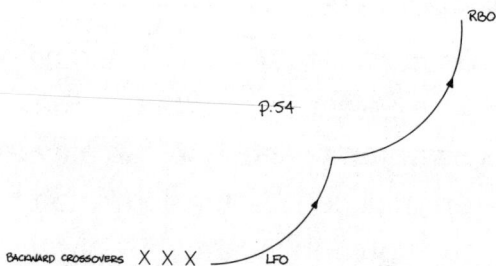

RBO

P.54

BACKWARD CROSSOVERS X X X ____ LFO

Approach a waltz jump by doing a few backward crossovers (see how handy they are to know?). Back crossovers build up your speed and you'll need good speed to lift your body up in the air and turn it around. From the back crossovers, you step onto a left forward outside edge. As you step forward, extend your right (or free) leg in back of you and angle both arms behind you. Your skating knee is bent, ready to spring. As you jump, you swing your free leg forward and up. At the same time, you "snap" or quickly bring your arms in front of your body, then overhead. Together, these two movements lift you into the air. Straighten the skating leg and extend both arms out to either side to make the half turn in the air. Then, prepare to land on your opposite leg (in this case, your right), traveling backward. Bend your right leg as you come down onto the ice, just as you learned in the bunny hop. Your free leg (now your left) should swing back. Your arms are at shoulder level, stretched out to either side.

The Salchow

The Swedish skater and former world champion Ulrich Salchow invented this graceful jump, one of Peggy's favorites. For this jump, you'll be turning a full turn or revolution in the air. This jump starts from a backward inside edge and ends on a backward inside edge of the opposite foot.

To approach the jump, start with a right forward outside edge, then do a drop three turn to get onto your left backward inside edge. To lift your body into the air, swing your free (right) foot in a wide, sweeping motion, counterclockwise, from behind your body to in front of it. Arms are at shoulder level, out to either side. Spring from the left foot, make one full turn in the air and land on a right backward inside edge. See Peggy's perfect landing, (photo 27). What's important to remember is that the action of the free leg gives you the power for the jump. The power increases when you move your arms along with the free leg, as a single unit. The jump can be sketched like this:

RBI

LBI

RBI

P. 55

DROP 3 TURN ——— RFO

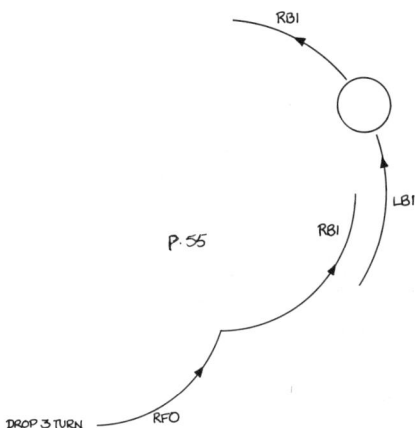

More advanced versions of the salchow are the Double Salchow and the Triple Salchow. That means that the skater must perform two (double) or three (triple) turns in the air before landing back on the ice. Peggy often included a double salchow in her routine.

The Loop

The Loop is known in Europe as the Rittberger, after its inventor. This jump calls for you to take off and land on the same foot, on the same edge, going the same direction. You must also do a full turn in the air.

The best way to start a loop jump is from a forward inside edge. For this example, let's say

you're approaching on a left forward inside edge.
Make a drop three turn and you'll be on a right
backward outside edge. Still skating backward,
get ready to jump. Your arms are at shoulder
level, your skating arm extended in back of you,
your free arm in front. Your free leg is in front of
your body, off the ice, following the curve that
your right skate is tracing. Bend your skating
knee to deepen the edge you're on. Jump up by
straightening your skating knee. Swing your free
leg up and around the skating leg. It looks like
you're trying to cross your legs in the air. As you
jump, your arms twist in different directions, helping you complete a full turn. Keep your body
upright during the jump. You'll land on your right
backward outside edge—the same leg, edge and
direction you jumped from. This is why the loop
is a tough jump to get right. The loop looks like
this:

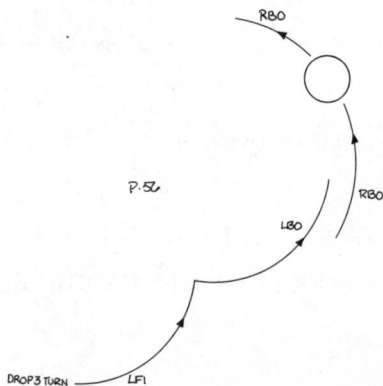

RBO

P. 5L

RBO

LBO

DROP 3 TURN — LFI

The Double Loop and the Triple Loop use the same basic positions as the loop. They differ only in the number of turns you make in the air. To do more than a single turn in the air, you'll need to practice getting higher and turning faster while you're off the ice.

The Toe Loop

The Toe Loop gets its name because you use the toe pick of the free foot like a vaulting pole in the process of the jump. This is the first of the toe jumps you'll be learning. For this jump, you take off from a backward outside edge. You use the toe pick of your free foot to hold the position before you actually leave the ice. The tapping of your toe pick into the ice should be part of a smooth movement. You should not come to a full stop when you touch your toe pick to the ice. An easy way to think of this jump is like a waltz jump off the toe, with one full revolution in the air.

From a left forward inside edge, do a drop three turn to approach the jump on a right backward outside edge. Extend your free leg out behind you, in line with your skating foot. Without any hesitation, place the toe pick of your free skate into the ice. Be sure to place your toe pick straight into the ice so that you will not slip or slide as you take off. Bring your skating leg toward the free leg, now anchored by the toe pick. Shift your weight to the toe pick, and kick your skating leg up to pull your body into the air. Do one full turn. You will land on the same edge, the right backward outside edge. As you land, extend your free leg in back of you. Your arms should be out to either side, at shoulder level. Here's a diagram of the toe loop:

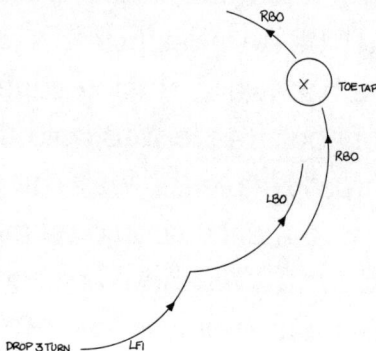

You can also do a Double Toe Loop and a Triple Toe Loop by completing two or three full revolutions in the air.

The Flip

The Flip is another toe jump. It is a jump with a full revolution in the air. You take off from a back inside edge turn and land on a back outside edge. The approach to the flip jump takes a great deal of practice. You begin skating on a forward outside edge, then do a drop three turn onto a backward inside edge on the other foot. Instead of curving naturally after you finish the drop three turn, you must use control and straighten your curve into a straight line. You're now on a left backward inside edge, your right (or free) leg extended behind you. Your skating arm is extended in back of you, your free arm is front of your body. Place the toe pick of your free foot (your right foot) into the ice. Draw the skating foot back toward the planted toe pick and spring into the air. As you rise, bring your skating arm forward to meet your free arm. Pull arms close to your chest as you rotate one full turn. During the rotation, your legs are parallel to each other and close together. You land on a back inside edge of the opposite or right foot. The flip looks like this:

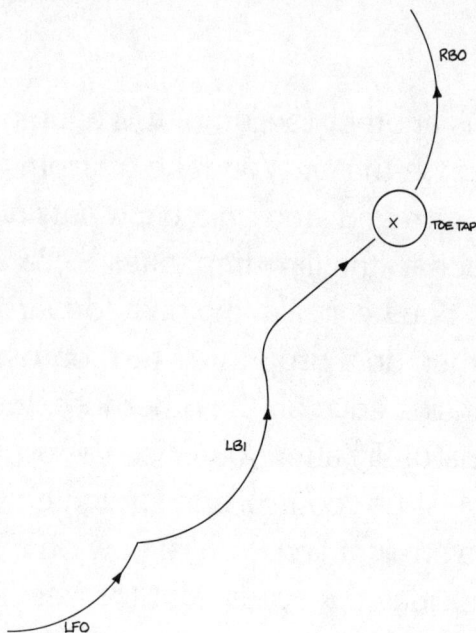

RBO

X TOE TAP

LBI

LFO

The Double Flip and then the Triple Flip are the advanced steps for the flip jump.

The Lutz

Named after its inventor, The Lutz is the most difficult of the one-revolution jumps. It involves a reverse jump in a counterclockwise direction. It is very similiar to the flip. The difference between the two is that you take off for the lutz on a back outside edge, instead of the flip's back inside edge. Approach the jump on a back outside edge from a series of back crossovers. Your free leg is extended in front of you. Your skating arm is raised and held in back of you, your free arm in front of you. Gradually move the free arm and leg to the back of your body and move the skating arm in front of you. Place the toe pick of your free foot into the ice and allow the skating foot to approach the planted toe pick. When you spring into the air, you are actually backing into the turn. Pull both arms toward your chest. The landing curves in a direction opposite to your takeoff—on a backward outside edge, on the opposite foot. Wondering what it looks like?

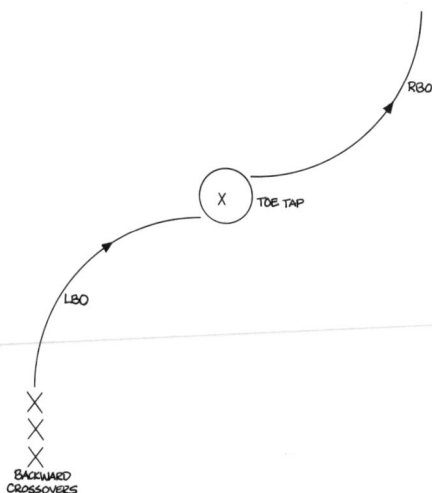

You can also perform Double and Triple Lutzes. Peggy performed a double lutz in her first U.S. National Novice Competition in 1963. She placed second—very good!

The Axel

Axel Paulson of Norway gave his name to this jump of his own invention—The Axel. It is a 1½-turn jump. The approach to the jump is on a forward outside edge, and the landing, on a backward outside edge on the opposite foot. The jump is basically a combination of the waltz jump (a one-half turn jump) and the loop jump (a one-turn jump). If you've learned both of these jumps, you can learn the axel. To do an axel, you leave the ice facing forward (just like the waltz jump) and then you turn in the air so that you land backward on the other foot, as in the loop jump. The leap up into the air resembles the waltz jump, but instead of doing just a half turn, you must make 1½ turns in the air. To summarize the moves in an axel jump:

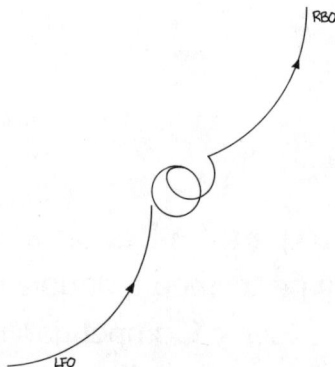

RBO

LFO

More advanced axel jumps include the Double Axel (2½ turns) and the Triple Axel (3½ turns). One of Peggy's most breath-taking moves is a distinctive combination of a spread eagle into an axel jump and after landing, back into the spread eagle. It is a move that she created herself. Peggy's originality and creativity with the basic moves are what made her a champion skater.

PART IV
YOUR SKATING FUTURE

CHAPTER 14

Getting Better—All The Time

Skating better—that's the aim of learning new moves, practicing old moves, putting together the old and the new. As you see yourself improving, you will start to set new goals for yourself. Some will be short-term goals. These are goals that you can reach with a few more lessons, or just some more hours of practice. Your short-term goal might be to jump higher so that you can do a double or a triple revolution jump; maybe you want to learn a new spin or look more graceful on the ice. Still other goals will be set for the future and are long-term goals. These long-term goals might include entering (and winning) skating competitions, or becoming part of the U.S. Figure Skating Team. You need all kinds of goals. The smaller steps that you reach with short-term

goals bring you that much closer to achieving the major step of a long-term goal.

How far you will go, and how long it will take you to get there, will depend on how much you want to make these dreams come true. Your success depends on your talent, your desire and the time you are willing to spend to improve. Giving up everything else just for skating is not really the answer. Peggy led a very balanced life, even when she was competing to be selected for the Olympics. She spent time with her family, she attended school, she went to the movies. She scheduled her skating lessons and practice sessions around her life, not the other way around. She used to skate before and after school, and sometimes she brought her books to the rink. She would read a bit, then skate a few laps and think about what she'd read!

Peggy's successes show what talent and a lot of hard work can do. When she won the Gold Medal for figure skating at the 1968 Winter Olympics, Peggy calculated that in 11 years of skating, she had practiced 20,000 hours. All that time, energy and practice got her to the Olym-

29. *Become A Skating Great Someday?*
   (from left to right: John Curry, Peggy Fleming,
   Dorothy Hamill, Robin Cousins)

pics—which was her dream. Her effort was worth it to her.

Perhaps your dreams don't include the Olympics, or maybe you're not very sure just what you want to do with your skating. Joining an ice show, entertaining people, becoming a skating teacher or just learning to skate well may all be possibilities, or distant dreams. Your dreams, whatever they are, are just as grand, just as important for you as anyone else's dreams. You're following Peggy's philosophy of skating: She often said that she didn't skate for anyone but herself. And she practiced only to get better, not to beat other people. If that's your attitude, then you'll come out a winner, too!

Checklist Of the Moves and Terms Covered in This Section

- Freestyle style
- Centering a Spin
- Two-Foot Spin
- One-Foot Spin
- Sit Spin
- Layback Spin
- Camel Spin
- Flying Spins
- Spin Combinations
- Bunny Hop
- Waltz Jump
- Salchow
- Loop
- Toe Loop
- Flip
- Lutz
- Axel